SPORTS REPORTS

Stories Behind the Headlines

Paul Romanuk

SCHOLASTIC CANADA LTD.

*With thanks to Dimitra Chronopoulos for her help
in researching these sports reports.*

Designed by Dennis Boyes

Canadian Cataloguing in Publication Data

Romanuk, Paul
    Sports reports : stories behind the headlines

ISBN 0-590-50020-1

1. Readers (Elementary). 2. Readers – Athletes – Canada – Biography.
3. Readers – Sports/ I. Title

PE1121.R65 1998   428.6   C98-931815-X

Copyright © 1999 by Paul Romanuk

5 4 3 2   Printed and bound in Canada   2/0

Contents

1867: New Brunswick Rowers Take the
World by Storm!   *1*

1954: Teenager Swims Lake Ontario!   *9*

1972: Team Canada Defeats the
Soviet Union!   *17*

1984: Canada Wins First Gold Medal
Awarded for New Olympic Sport!   *25*

1989: Stemmle Defeats Killer Course!   *33*

1992: Blue Jays Win World Series! *41*

1992: Canadian Women First in
       Paralympics! *49*

1994: Gretzky Beats Howe's
       Lifetime Record! *57*

1996: Another Gold for Heddle
       and McBean! *65*

1996: Donovan Bailey Fastest Man
       in the World *73*

1997: Ted Nolan Wins Coach
       of the Year! *81*

1867

New Brunswick Rowers Take the World by Storm!

In the 1800s, sports became more organized than they had been up to that time. Many of our modern competitions began then.

One sport that became more organized was rowing. One of the first major rowing competitions ever held took place in 1829. It was a contest between teams from Oxford and Cambridge universities in England. Since then, that race has become one of the biggest annual rowing events.

In the mid and late 1800s, rowing was one of the most popular sports in the world. It was very big in Canada. The people in Saint John, New Brunswick, believed that their top crew had some of the best rowers to be found anywhere.

The crew members were three fishermen and a lighthouse keeper. The fishermen were Samuel Hutton, Robert Fulton and George Price. The lighthouse keeper was Elijah Ross. Hutton and Ross had been rowing together since 1862. Fulton joined them a couple of years later. Price was the final person to join the crew.

The year 1867 was a special one in New Brunswick. It was the year of Confederation. New Brunswick and Nova Scotia had just joined with Upper and Lower Canada to form a brand new country called Canada. During the celebrations, someone got the idea of sending the Saint John crew to the World's Fair in Paris.

World's Fairs were huge events in the 1800s. It took place over about six months, hosted by a different city each year. There were displays for the arts, science and

industry. People came from all over the world to see and take part in the event.

Some sports groups began to hold their competitions in the same city where a World's Fair was taking place. They knew that would bring attention to their sport. And it was easier to draw athletes to a city where there was already a major event under way.

The French often hosted World Fairs. In 1867 they hosted one in Paris. It was one of the biggest the world had ever seen. Along with many other events, it included the World Amateur Rowing Championships.

In Paris, the Saint John crew would be able to compete against some of the top rowers in the world. "Our crew can beat any other crew!" people said. "And there's a big cash prize for the winners."

The problem was that Paris was a long way from Saint John. It would cost a lot for the crew to get there. But the idea of competing in Paris was important to the people in Saint John and the rest of New Brunswick. So, together, the people and the government raised $6000 to send the crew to France.

The four men packed up their boat, their gear and some personal belongings and headed for Paris. That city was like no place they had ever been. They stared in awe at the old buildings, the narrow streets, the sidewalk cafés, the crowds of people. Paris was a lot bigger than Saint John — or any other city in the young country that was Canada.

There would be two races. The first course had a sharp turn in it. The second one was straight. There were five other boats in each race. The other crews were from all over Europe. One was from London, England, one from Germany, one from Paris.

When it came time to race, the St. John crew looked at the other crews in wonder. They had sleek, modern boats. They had splendid uniforms in the colours of their country or their rowing club. They also had a coxswain — a person who sits in the boat, steers and calls out instructions to keep the crew rowing together stroke by stroke.

By comparison, the Saint John crew looked almost comical. They wore black trousers held up by braces. They had flesh-coloured shirts and pink caps to keep the sun off their heads. Their boat was much heavier than the other boats. One of the crew members steered it with his feet while he was rowing.

The Canadian crew noticed something else about the other crews as well. They used a different rowing style. The European rowers used long strokes. The Saint John crew preferred to use shorter, quicker strokes.

People wondered how this clumsy-looking crew from Canada, with their silly uniforms and their strange rowing style, could possibly compete. They were in for a surprise.

In the first race, the Saint John crew took the lead early. They won so easily that Robert Fulton couldn't resist having a little fun as they rowed across the finish line in front of the crowd. He took off his pink cap and waved while he continued to row with one hand!

The Canadian crew won the second race just as easily. They crossed the finish line three boat-lengths in front. That made them the World Amateur Rowing Champions.

Their prize was 3000 French francs — about $750 in Canadian money. That was a lot of money in 1867!

Word of their win soon reached Canada. The city of Saint John organized a parade and a party to welcome "the Paris Crew" back home. Thousands of people came out to greet the four men when they arrived. Bands played and people cheered. Fireworks lit the sky. The mayor presented the Paris Crew with a cash prize of $500.

History doesn't record whether or not the crew bought new uniforms with their prize money. But it really didn't matter how they looked — they rowed like champions!

1954
Teenager Swims Lake Ontario!

Late in the evening of September 8, 1954, 16-year-old Marilyn Bell stood looking out eagerly at the dark waters of Lake Ontario. She was about to cross the lake in a marathon swim that would make history.

Marathon swimming was very popular in the 1950s. Long-distance swims were almost always held outdoors, in a lake or an ocean. Marilyn was trying to become the first person ever to swim across Lake Ontario.

She had always loved the water and could already swim when she was four. By the time she was 14, she was giving swimming lessons. What she liked best was teaching disabled children how to swim. She watched them learn to relax. She felt good when they began to move about easily in the water.

Marilyn was more at home in the water than on land. Since swimming is great exercise, before long Marilyn was in top shape. She decided to test herself in a marathon swim.

In July, 1954, she entered the famous Atlantic City Marathon swim. She had no trouble passing that test. She was the first woman ever to finish the race.

That same summer, the Canadian National Exhibition (CNE) in Toronto offered a $10 000 prize to an American swimmer, Florence Chadwick. If she could swim across Lake Ontario, she would win the money. Her swim would start in Youngstown, New York. It would finish in Toronto, at the shore of the CNE grounds. The distance was about 51 kilometres.

The idea excited Canadians. But many wondered why the CNE had offered the

prize to an American swimmer. Didn't
Canada have some of the finest marathon
swimmers in the world? News of the swim
spread. Both Marilyn Bell and Winnie Roach
Leuszler decided to swim the lake too, "for
the honour of Canada." Suddenly, the event
had turned into a race.

That's why Marilyn was standing on the
shore of Lake Ontario this September night.
Florence Chadwick had already entered the
water. Marilyn and Winnie Roach Leuszler
were preparing to follow her.

In a boat offshore were Marilyn's parents,
a doctor and a nurse, a few friends and her

coach, Gus Ryder. They watched as Marilyn and Winnie joined Florence in the dark water. The three swimmers were on their way to Toronto. The race was on!

Marilyn's hours of training paid off quickly. After only five kilometres, her strong strokes carried her past the other two women. Five hours after the race began, she had a big lead. Now came the tough part — the race against herself. She still had a long way to go and she would have to do it alone. There would be no other swimmers near her.

As Marilyn got farther out into the lake, the water started to get colder and rougher. It was hard to swim through the waves without being dragged off course. She was getting weaker. She had to work hard not to fall asleep. Now and then she could feel fish brushing up against her. Eels tried to stick themselves to her body.

Through it all, her friends and family cheered her on from the boat. Her coach wrote notes on a blackboard and held it over the side for her to read. She was getting very tired, but she kept going.

As she swam towards Toronto, thousands of people across Canada were listening to the radio. Radio stations gave a report every hour. Newspapers printed thousands of extra copies and extra editions. By Thursday afternoon, people had started to gather on the Toronto lakeshore near the CNE grounds. They wanted to welcome Marilyn when she arrived.

Back out on the lake, Marilyn was doing all she could to finish. She was near the end of her strength, and the wind and waves kept pushing her off course. She had to stop several times to float and rest. The other two women had already dropped out of the race because they were too sick and tired to keep going. Florence was pulled from the water after 26 kilometres. Winnie came out at the 32 kilometre mark.

The race was Marilyn's to win. All she had to do was finish. She knew she could do it! She just had to keep going. She wanted to climb into the boat, wrap herself in a nice warm blanket and sip on a hot cup of soup. But she couldn't. She swam on towards Toronto, getting closer and closer.

Finally, she could see the shore. She could also see hundreds — no, thousands! — of people. Some were sitting, and some were standing. But they were all cheering for her! She kept swimming towards the shore. At last, she waded out of the water. She had done it! She was the first person ever to swim across Lake Ontario.

Marilyn had made the trip in 20 hours and 59 minutes. She had spent almost a whole night and day in the water, without stopping! Her picture was on the front page of almost every newspaper in Canada, and the CNE gave her the $10 000 prize.

Teenager Swims Lake Ontario!

The swim made Marilyn famous at the age of 16. The people of Toronto lined the streets to cheer her. People all across Canada wanted to talk to her and ask her questions. She got thousands of cards and letters. And she got lots of gifts, including a car.

A year later, in July, Marilyn became the youngest swimmer ever to cross the English Channel. In August, 1956, she swam across the Strait of Juan de Fuca off the coast of British Columbia. Shortly after that, she decided to retire from marathon swimming.

Marilyn Bell became a teacher. And if any of her students asked what she used to do in her summer vacations, she always had a great story to tell!

1972
Team Canada Defeats the Soviet Union!

There are some sporting events that are more than just sporting events. One such event took place in September, 1972. It was an eight-game hockey series between the best Canadian and the best Soviet (Russian) Russian players. This event aroused strong feelings. Millions of people on both sides of the world were caught up in the excitement.

In 1972, the two greatest hockey countries were Canada and what was then the Soviet Union. The National Hockey League (NHL) was the best professional hockey league in the world. And almost all of its players had been born in Canada.

But in world competition, the Soviets were tops. Their players were classed as non-professional, since they weren't paid for playing hockey. Even though they were full-time hockey players, they were paid as officers in the Soviet army.

According to the rules of the day, as long as you weren't being paid to play a sport, you weren't classed as a professional. Canada's best hockey players were being paid by the NHL. So they couldn't play in the World Championship series or the Olympics.

The teams Canada had to send to those events almost always lost to the more skilled Soviet teams. Canadian hockey fans thought they should be able to send a team made up of their best players — players from the NHL. If they could do that, they believed, they would win.

The hockey fans finally got their wish in 1972. There would be a "Summit Series" of eight games between the Soviet National Team and a Canadian team made up of NHL players. Most Canadian fans expected

Team Canada Defeats the Soviet Union!

Canada to win every game of the series. There was no possible way the Soviets could defeat Canada's best. But they were in for a surprise!

The first game of the series was played in Montreal on September 2, 1972. It was a warm fall day and the Forum was packed with thousands of happy fans. They were ready for a Canadian victory. In the crowd was Canadian Prime Minister Pierre Trudeau.

The fans were on their feet as soon as the game started. Boston Bruins star Phil Esposito had skated to the Soviet net and scored. It was 1-0 for Canada only 30 seconds into the game! Six minutes later, Paul Henderson scored for Canada. He made a great shot from a face-off in the Soviet zone. It was 2-0 for Canada. A win was in the bag!

Not quite.

Before long, the Soviets started to skate and pass and move the puck better than the

Canadians were doing. They tied the score before the end of the first period. By the end of the second period, they had a 4-2 lead. In the third period, the Soviets scored three more goals. Canada lost 7-3. The fans in the Forum and the millions of people watching on TV were stunned. How could Canada's best players be defeated like that?

They played the second game at Maple Leaf Gardens in Toronto. Canada won 4-1. Game three in Winnipeg was a 4-4 tie. The

fourth game was in Vancouver. Soviet goalie
Vladislav Tretiak played an outstanding
game. Canada lost 5-3. The fans booed the
players off the ice at the end of the game.

Now the Soviets led the series with two
wins, one loss and one tie. To win, Canada
would have to take three of the last four
games. The series moved to Moscow in the
Soviet Union. Canadian fans felt as if
something had been taken away from them.
Hockey wasn't "their" game anymore.

Canada lost game five. They had a 4-1
lead early in the third period. But the Soviets
came back with four goals in the final 15
minutes and won the game 5-4. Now Canada
had to win every one of the last three games.
Not many people thought they could do it.

The next three games were thrilling.
In game six, Canada built up a 3-1 lead and
hung on to win 3-2. In game seven, Paul
Henderson scored the winning goal with just
over two minutes left. A Soviet player pulled

him down, but he slid towards the goal and scored. Canada won the game 4-3 and tied the series.

Over 16 million Canadians watched the final game. Schools and businesses closed for the day. Everywhere, people crowded around television sets to watch.

In this game, the players on both teams gave everything they had. They knew this was it. The game drove back and forth from end to end. It was one of the greatest hockey games ever played.

After two periods, the Soviets led 5-3. Canada needed to score three goals in the final period to win the series. Fighting hard, they tied the score at 5-5. But the game was almost over. It looked as if that's how it would end.

Then, in the final minute, Phil Esposito passed the puck in front of the net to Paul Henderson. Henderson took a shot. Tretiak made the save. Henderson took another shot.

Everyone watching the game gasped. The puck had crossed the goal line!

Any sports fan over the age of 35 can tell you exactly where he or she was when Henderson scored "the goal." There were only 34 seconds left on the clock. Canada held on and won the game 6-5. They also won the series. They had four wins, three losses and one tie.

Since "the series," the Soviets (now the Russians) and Canada have met several times. They always give the fans a great game. But no other series has captured the attention of so many people. Fans still think of those eight amazing games they played in September, 1972, as the best ever!

1984

Canada Wins First Gold Medal
Awarded for New Olympic Sport!

Many sports fans looked forward to the 1984
Summer Olympic Games in Los Angeles.
But they didn't really know what to expect.
Some changes were under way.

In the first place, athletes from the
Soviet Union wouldn't be there. They were
caught in the middle of a political conflict
between the United States and the Soviet
Union. They had been ordered to stay away
from the Olympics. As a result, many of the
top athletes in the world weren't in Los
Angeles.

Also, 15 new events were added for the
1984 Olympics. Sports fans were curious
about these new events. Among them was

rhythmic gymnastics. And with that event came a new Canadian star — Lori Fung.

Rhythmic gymnastics is a women's sport. Most people had never heard of it in 1984. Many didn't even think of it as a sport. How could routines that involved ribbons and hoops and balls be a sport?

But those people missed the mark. Sports are activities that work both mind and muscles. Rhythmic gymnastics certainly requires both. So it must be classed as a sport. "People who think that rhythmic gymnastics isn't a sport should step into the gym once or twice," says Lori Fung.

Rhythmic gymnasts use five different pieces of "equipment": ball, hoop, ribbon, rope and clubs. The routine for each of these items lasts about a minute and a half. The athletes are judged on technical merit, artistic merit and execution.

"Technical merit" takes into account how difficult the moves are. "Artistic merit"

depends on how appealing the whole routine is. "Execution" refers to how well the gymnast performs. To be good, these athletes must be strong. Their bodies must bend easily. They must be graceful and move smoothly. In other words, it's not as easy as it looks!

Lori started out and performed well as a regular gymnast. She liked the floor routines, and she liked to dance. When she was about 14, one of her teachers introduced her to rhythmic gymnastics. She liked those routines even better.

She moved ahead quickly. By the time she was 16, she had earned a spot on the national team. That meant she had the best coaches in Canada. It also meant she could travel and compete in other countries. At the World Championships in 1981, she finished in 30th place. This was the best showing ever by a North American.

As she travelled, Lori saw that people in other countries paid more attention to her sport than Canadians did. They came out in large numbers to watch the athletes and cheer them on. As a result, more young athletes took up the sport. And because more people were interested, more time and money were spent for coaching and training.

To be tops in her sport, Lori knew she would have to get the best coaching and training she could. She spent a month in Bulgaria in 1983 and a month in Romania in 1984. She trained with some of the best coaches and athletes in the world. In

Canada Wins First Gold Medal Awarded for New Olympic Sport!

Romania, Doina Staiculescu was her training partner. Later they competed against each other.

Lori spent many hours every day at the gym. She worked on all of the little things that make a routine as good as it can be. She knew that the judging at the Olympics would be tough. She wanted to be at her best.

She had to finish in the top 50 at the 1983 World Championships to be able to go to the Olympics. Because of all her hard work, she finished in 23rd place. That was her best showing ever. She was off to the Olympics!

This was the first time a rhythmic gymnastics competition was held during the Olympics. Nobody expected Lori to win. She wasn't even in the top ten at the World Championships. Why would anyone think she might win Olympic gold?

But Lori's quick thinking gave her a chance. In the ribbon routine, the ribbon can't touch the floor or the body of the athlete. If it does, the judges take points off. While Lori was practising, she noticed that the air conditioner in the gym was making her ribbon swirl. She decided she'd have to do something about it.

Here's how she explained her plan. "Everyone was saying, 'Oh, well, the air conditioner. We'll just have to deal with it, accept it.' But I decided in the change room that I wasn't going to accept it. I wanted a 9.7 and I wasn't going to accept an 8.5 just because the air conditioner might create problems." So Lori changed her whole routine.

She stayed on one side of the floor, where she could control the ribbon more easily. Doina Staiculescu didn't do that. As a result, her ribbon twisted around her back and touched the floor. Losing so many points probably cost her the gold medal. But it opened the door for Lori. As Doina left the floor in tears, Lori tried to relax and prepare for her next routine.

"I was in shock," she said later. "She came off in tears. I thought it was terrible, but I wondered suddenly: where am I in the standings? All I knew was that I was somewhere up there in the top five." Doina was still in the lead. Lori knew it would be close.

Lori finished her hoop routine and waited for the judges to post her score. Suddenly, there it was on the scoreboard. The gold medal total read: *Lori Fung, CHINA, 57.950 points.*

Wait a minute! China? That's right. The people working the scoreboard weren't quite as sharp as Lori was that day.

But it didn't matter what the scoreboard said. Lori's hard work and quick thinking had won a gold medal for Canada — the first Olympic gold medal ever awarded in rhythmic gymnastics!

1989
Stemmle Defeats Killer Course!

A ski racer can travel up to 140 kilometres an hour. Ski racing is a sport for people who like to take chances. It requires the nerves of a bomb disposal expert. One missed turn, one unexpected bump, and things can get horribly out of control.

For those reasons, and more, the sport is a perfect match for Brian Stemmle. He is one of the finest downhill skiers ever to come out of Canada.

Brian caught the eyes of the coaches at a national team training camp when he was only 16 years old. He was quickly named to a special junior team. This team would allow him to learn from the best coaches in Canada.

What the coaches saw was a very talented young athlete who still needed to learn the importance of hard work and dedication. Brian wasn't the first person in that position. Former national ski team head coach Glen Wurtele recalls that "Like so many other naturally talented people, Brian never had to work very hard to be good. It didn't matter what you threatened him with. It didn't matter how tough you were with him. He wouldn't work any harder than he thought he should."

Less than two years after he joined the special team, Brian captured the United States downhill championship. During the spring of 1985, he skied in his first World Cup race. And by the 1987 season, he seemed to be ready to win any race he entered.

The 1988 Calgary Olympics were coming up. Things were looking great for Brian and the Canadian men's downhill ski

team. Just two months before the Olympics, Brian finished in third place on a tough World Cup course in Italy. His teammate, Rob Boyd, finished first. Then, just before the Olympics began, Brian injured his knee. He was forced to watch from the sidelines.

The next season, Brian was skiing well when the tour moved into Austria. Austria is the home of one of the most famous World Cup downhill races. The Hahnenkamm is the kind of course Brian loves to ski on — fast, dangerous and tough. It takes a special kind of skier to win on a hill like this. Those who succeed take great pride in winning on what many people think is the toughest downhill course in the world.

The race attracts thousands of people every year. People come from hundreds of kilometres away to watch skiers battle their way down the course.

First comes "The Mousetrap." This jump has to be taken at high speed from a short turn to the left. Skiers have to get control of their skis quickly as they come out of the turn so they can set themselves up for the jump.

Next comes a steep hill that is almost always iced over. The race can be won here if a skier builds up enough speed. But too much speed can end in a crash.

Finally, after several slopes and curves, the skiers come to a wide left-hand turn. It's followed by a big fall-away jump. Here, too, skiers have to make sure they have enough speed, but not too much, as they head into the jump.

Some of the greatest skiers have made their mark on this course. It has also claimed several victims. Among those are Canadians Steve Podborski, Dave Murray and Todd Brooker. Podborski crashed when he lost control on a turn. Murray's knee flew up and knocked him on the chin. The blow was so hard that he suffered a head injury! Brooker wiped out when he lost a ski near the end of the run. The crash ended his career.

Now it was January 14, 1989. Brian Stemmle stood in the starting gate and looked down the course. He had had trouble with it during training. He knew it would be just as tough today. It was -4°C. The course was icy and very fast. The timer beeped and the gate flashed open.

Brian was the 24th skier out of the gate. His run was going well. He was heading towards the steep, icy part of the course.

Then he swept into the last turn just a little too wide. He could feel himself getting too close to the safety net. He tried to correct his course, but was thrown off balance by a bump. He couldn't work his skies back up the hill. He was in big trouble.

Brian became snagged in the net. He was nearly ripped in two as he went from over 100 kilometres an hour to zero in a fraction of a second. He was thrown into the air, out of control. He crashed onto the hard ice, landing on his shoulder and back. He skidded across the ice into another safety net 100 metres farther down the course.

Medics were on the scene quickly. They found Brian conscious but in shock. They took him by helicopter to a nearby hospital so doctors could see how badly he was injured. They found a fractured pelvis and many internal injuries.

The doctors operated on Brian twice within the first 24 hours after the accident.

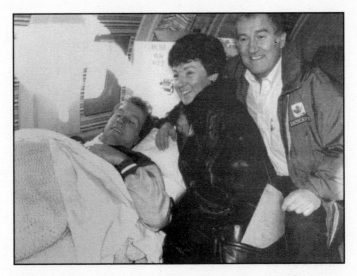

A machine helped him to breathe. Medicines kept him asleep for four days to help him cope with the pain.

When they could move him, Canadian doctors took him back home for more surgery. They believed he would recover from his injuries and go on to live a normal life. But it looked as though his skiing career was finished.

No matter what others thought or said, Brian was determined to return to downhill racing. He worked for months to help his body mend. The process was painful and slow. As he said a few years later, "It taught me what work was really about."

One year later, he was back training with the Canadian National Ski Team. Returning to World Cup racing was still a long way off. But he was starting to see the results of his months of hard work.

Only 20 months after the crash, Brian entered and won the downhill event at the Pan-Am Winter Games. Almost two years after the accident, he returned to the World Cup for a race in France. Amazingly, he finished in 10th place! Everyone marvelled at his comeback.

In 1994, five years after his crash, Brian returned to face the course he had defeated. He didn't make headlines that year. But most people agree that, just by being there, Brian proved himself a champion!

1992
Blue Jays Win World Series!

At the end of each baseball season, the league champions have always played against each other in the World Series. But for 89 years, "world" just meant the United States. In 1992, the American League champions came from another country — Canada. That year the Toronto Blue Jays played the Atlanta Braves in the World Series.

For Canadian fans, the 1992 series was the end of a wait that had begun on a snowy afternoon 15 years before. The Blue Jays played their first game ever on April 7, 1977. Both the team and the fans enjoyed that first game, in spite of the snow — or perhaps because of it. In the end, the Blue Jays won 9-5 over the Chicago White Sox.

It was a good start. But the Jays didn't follow up with too many wins in the early years. They were always at the bottom of their division. They were last in the league in wins, batting and pitching. Not until 1983 did they finally have a year with more wins than losses.

In 1985 the Jays won their division and played in the championship series for the first time. But they lost to Kansas City in seven games. They got that far again in 1989 and 1991, but both times they lost. In 1989 they lost to the Oakland Athletics in five games. In 1991 they lost to the Minnesota Twins.

In 1992 things got better for the Blue Jays and their fans. Over four million people came to the Skydome to watch them play. Leading the team were some of the greatest stars in the league. Six players drove in over 60 runs each. Dave Winfield batted in 108 runs. Pitcher Jack Morris won 21 games and lost only six. Toronto came first in the division and won over Oakland in six games in the championship series.

But could the team continue to win in the final round of the playoffs? Could they meet the final test — the World Series?

The Blue Jays became Canada's team, not just Toronto's. People all across the country watched the games on TV. In Canada, hockey is usually king. But that summer Canada became a baseball nation.

Not one of the Blue Jays had been born in Canada, but the country made them all "honorary Canadians."

Two home runs decided the first game of the series. One in the fourth inning gave the Jays a 1-0 lead. Then Atlanta hit one that scored three runs in the sixth inning. The final score was 3-1.

In the second game, first one team was on top, then the other. Toronto finally won 5-4. This time the win came with a two-run homer over the left-field wall in the ninth inning.

It was a thrilling game. But what people in Canada were talking about the next day was what happened before the game. During the playing of "O Canada," the Canadian flag was carried onto the field upside down! It was an honest mistake. The people in Atlanta thought that way was right. "Leaves hang upside down when they're on the tree," they pointed out. But they apologized.

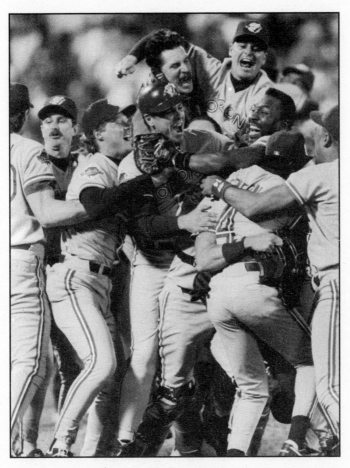

Game three was played in Toronto. That was the first time a World Series game had ever been played outside the United States.

It was a magic night. Inside the Skydome nearly 52 000 people watched and cheered.

The Jays won in the ninth inning when a single-base hit scored the winning run. But the best play of the game — maybe of the entire series — happened in the fourth inning. The Braves had two men on base and none out. What looked like another homer sailed towards the fence. Toronto's Devon White raced for it. When he reached the fence, he leaped into the air, stretching as high as he could. His glove found the ball just before he crashed into the wall. He hit so hard that he left the shape of his body in the padding. "It was the greatest catch I've ever made," he said later.

Game four was close too. It was the third game in a row that the Blue Jays won by only one run. Their pitchers were great. This time it was third baseman Kelly Gruber who made a great play. As the ball came towards him along the ground, he ran and

grabbed it with his bare hand. He threw it to
first base to make the out.

Now the Blue Jays needed only one
more victory to win the World Series.
Everybody was ready for a Toronto win in
game five. In fact, some people were too
ready. News of a victory parade came out
before the game even started! Over 52 000
fans were ready to celebrate as soon as the
Toronto pitcher made his way to the mound.

The Braves scored a run in the first
inning. Toronto scored too, and the two
teams stayed tied until the fifth inning. Then
an Atlanta player hit a grand-slam home run.
So the Jays didn't win game five after all. The
series returned to Atlanta for game six.

The sixth game lasted over four hours. It
went into extra innings when the Braves tied
the game at 2-2 in the ninth inning. There
were no runs scored in the 10th. Then, in
the 11th inning, Toronto's Dave Winfield
sent a double over third base. It flew into the

left field corner, scoring runners from second and first. The Braves got one run back, but it wasn't enough.

For the final out, Toronto pitcher Mike Timlin picked up a bunted ball and tossed it to first base. The Toronto Blue Jays had won Canada's first World Series title! Dave Winfield was the hero of the game. "America's game is going to Canada for a while," he told reporters after the game.

Back in Toronto, close to half a million people danced in the streets. They welcomed the Jays home with a huge parade through the city to the Skydome.

And then came the moment the fans had all been waiting for — the World Series Championship banner was raised high above the field. It looked right at home up there next to the Canadian flag!

1992
Canadian Women First in Paralympics!

Some athletes aren't as strong as others in body or in skill. But they can make up for that if they are eager and clever. The women's wheelchair basketball team that won the Barcelona Paralympic gold medal in 1992 is a great example. Canada didn't have the best players. But, together, those players made the best team.

In 1992, there were 17 players in the national program for women's wheelchair basketball. They usually played together just three weeks during the year. But that year was special.

Coach Tim Frick and his staff selected the 12 best players in the program to make up Canada's team for the Paralympics. They would get to train together for six weeks.

Tim knew that, to win, the women would have to prepare themselves mentally. Theirs wouldn't be the most skilled team at the games. Most people expected them to finish anywhere from third to fifth. The two teams to beat were from Germany and the United States. Both of those teams had beaten Canada two years earlier at the Gold Cup World Championships.

The team got together in Edmonton for a week-long camp to pick the players who would go to Barcelona. The decisions weren't easy. Chantal Benoit was good on offense. Marni Abbott was a good leader and would motivate the others. Linda Kutrowski would offer patience and attention to detail. The team would be an interesting mix. But was it the right mix to win gold?

After Tim had chosen the team, the players started to prepare for the games. In

Canadian Women First in Paralympics!

May, they got together in Ottawa for two weeks. They trained again for two weeks in July. And they had another week together in Germany just before the games started.

During their training in Canada, the team competed against able-bodied athletes who had learned to use wheelchairs. "This gave us top-class competition every day in the training camps," Tim says.

The players also spent hours watching video tapes of the teams they would be playing against. And they thought and talked a lot about what it would take to win. "We knew we weren't as fast or as skilled as the top teams," explains Tim. "But we decided we could be better prepared mentally."

The team members talked with one another about their goals. They talked about controlling their emotions in tough situations. And, most of all, they talked about enjoying themselves. "We loved every moment," Tim recalls.

Canada would begin against a weak Spanish team. But they knew they would also have some tough games. They would have to play against Germany and Australia in the first round.

They opened up against Spain with a 59-8 win. It's not polite to embarrass another team. But it was important for Canada to put up as many points as they could in the game against Spain. They might need those points to make the next round if this round ended in a tie. The decision would be based on their points for and against.

Their second game was against Australia. It was another win for Canada, by a score of 35-30.

The final game in round one was much more difficult. It was against Germany, and the Germans were tough. They didn't give Canada any chance to relax or slow down the speed of the game. It was then that Tim's efforts to get his team mentally prepared paid off. In spite of the pressure, Canada didn't crack. They won the game 29-28.

Next was a semi-final game against the Netherlands. Canada had defeated this team two years earlier at the Gold Cup World Championships to win a bronze medal. They were a tough team too. But they depended on one or two key players.

Canada's plan was to put pressure on their top player. They stayed close to her and made her work for every point. The plan succeeded. The player became tired and frustrated. In the end, she couldn't do anything. Canada won the game 46-43. The team had earned a place in the final!

The final game was against the United States. Everyone thought the US team would win. But once again the Canadian team's mental toughness and their ability to carry out their game plan paid off.

Tim knew that his players had to get off to a fast start. If they fell behind early, the US

team could put Canada in a hole that would be hard to dig out of. But the opposite happened. Canada jumped into an eight point lead right from the beginning. And they continued to take charge of the play. The pressure started to tell on the Americans.

"When we got to the final, we had nothing to lose," Tim explains. "The USA had their title to lose. A silver would have been just as good for us."

The Americans had not trailed late in a game in over four years — and they were playing like it. No matter what they tried, Canada broke up the play. Canada's defence was strong. They took shots every chance they got. When time ran out, the Canadians were ahead. Their 35-26 win stunned the USA.

"In reality," says Tim, "the tournament was won in our minds a year earlier. That's when we first began to dream. That's when we began to believe that if everything fell into place, and if every break went our way, then maybe we could win the gold."

The Canadian players believed in themselves. They were mentally prepared. They were focused. Their win is proof that sometimes the biggest weapon athletes have isn't their strength or size. It's what's between their ears!

Gretzky Beats Howe's Lifetime Record!

Wayne Gretzky's hockey career started the same way thousands of other Canadian hockey careers have started — on a backyard rink. Like many other parents, Walter Gretzky thought it would be a great idea to build a rink in the backyard for his kids to skate on. For Walter, a rink in the backyard meant that Wayne could play hockey and he could keep an eye on the boy without leaving his warm kitchen. A great idea. One shared by many parents to this day!

But the similarity between Gretzky's career and others that began on a backyard rink ends right there. Wayne has dominated hockey more than any other player in the history of the game.

At the beginning of the 1998-99 season, Wayne held or shared 61 individual National Hockey League (NHL) records. He has won the NHL scoring title 10 times. He has won the Hart Trophy as the Most Valuable Player nine times. He has been a member of a Stanley Cup Championship team four times. And he still loves playing hockey as much as he did all those years ago in his backyard.

"I love playing the game," Wayne has said many times. "All the other things that go on in my career take second place to the amount of fun I have when I'm out there on the rink playing the game."

Wayne's talent for the game put him ahead of the pack right from the start. As a 10-year-old playing minor hockey in his home town of Brantford, he scored 378 goals in 82 games! By the time he was 14, he was competing against players up to 20 years old. He still dominated.

When he was 16, Wayne was drafted by the Sault Ste. Marie Greyhounds of the Ontario Hockey League (OHL). It was there that his number became the now famous 99. He had always worn number 9. That was the number his boyhood hero, Gordie Howe, wore. But that number was already being used by another player on the team.

"You can't wear one 9," the coach told him. "So wear two."

But hockey teams didn't use 99 as a number. Wayne worried that the other players would think he was showing off. "They'll be running at me all night," he said.

"The way you play they'll be running at you anyway," the coach pointed out.

In 1977-78, Wayne finished second in league scoring with 182 points (70 goals and 112 assists) in 64 games. He was named OHL Rookie of the Year. He was ready for the next step in his young hockey career. And his timing was perfect.

At that time the World Hockey Association (WHA) was trying to compete with the NHL. It was trying to make a name

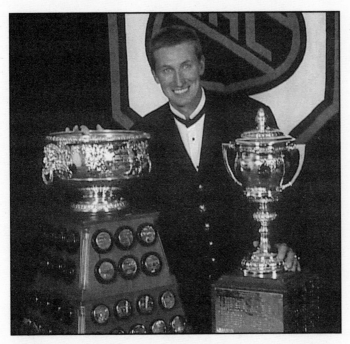

for itself by signing some of the best young players before the NHL could.

Wayne was the greatest young player in the game. Signing him would be a big deal for the league. Two teams approached him. He ended up signing a personal services contract for $850 000 with the owner of the Indianapolis Racers.

Wayne scored his first professional goal on October 22, 1978. But he played only eight games for the Racers before he was traded to the Edmonton Oilers. At that time the Oilers were a WHA team. Wayne ended his first, and only, season in the WHA with 110 points (46 goals, 64 assists) in 80 games. Again he was voted Rookie of the Year.

During the off-season, the WHA folded. Four of the teams joined the NHL, including the Edmonton Oilers. The stage was set for the most remarkable NHL career of all time.

In nine seasons with Edmonton, Wayne scored a total of 1669 regular-season points. He led the team to four Stanley Cup Championships. And he set several NHL records:

- He scored 92 goals during the 1981-82 season, 50 of them in only 39 games!
- From the beginning of the 1983-84 season, he scored at least one point in 51 games in a row.

- In the 1985-86 season, he had 163 assists and 215 total points.

The summer of 1988 brought two major changes to Wayne's life:

- On July 16, he married American actress Janet Jones. The wedding took place in Edmonton. Canadians from coast to coast wished the couple happiness.
- On August 9, Edmonton traded Wayne to the Los Angeles Kings. The deal shocked those same Canadians. How could the Oilers trade the greatest player in the game?

Despite the national outcry, the deal was done. The Greatest was now a King. He spent most of the next eight seasons with that team. During that time, the Kings made it to the Stanley Cup final only once. They never won the big prize.

But Wayne continued to pile up personal awards. Two of those were extra special:

- He became the all-time NHL points leader on October 15, 1989. This broke the record of 1851 points held by Gordie Howe.
- On March 23, 1994, he broke Howe's record of 801 career goals. At the age of 32, and with many years still to go in his career, he had more total goals and points than any other player in the history of the game.

When he scored the go-ahead goal, Wayne had a big smile on his face. He was no longer a boy. He had a wife and children and all the other things that go with being an adult. But his smile was the same as the one he smiled when he scored his first goal on the rink his father built back home in Brantford!

1996
Another Gold for Heddle and McBean!

One day in 1985, in her home in Toronto, Marnie McBean was watching a movie about rowing. She thought it was a sport she would enjoy. So she went to a local rowing club and signed up for a course. She was a natural rower. One year later she came home from the World Junior Rowing Championships with a bronze medal around her neck.

That same year, the coach of the rowing team at the University of British Columbia was talking to Kathleen Heddle. He wanted her to join the team. She decided to give it a try. It wasn't long before the national team noticed her.

Kathleen and Marnie both joined the national team in 1987. They were teammates, but on different crews. Sometimes they were part of a team of four rowers. Sometimes they were part of an eight-person team. But their coach wanted them to row together as a pair.

At first they weren't sure they wanted to be partners. They had both been thinking of rowing with someone else. But they decided to follow their coach's advice.

They quickly became good friends and a very successful team. They won gold medals in the pairs event at the World Championships in 1991 and at the Olympics in 1992. They also won Olympic gold with the team of eight.

In just five years, Kathleen and Marnie had won everything there was to win together. Many rowers compete for much longer without as much success. For Kathleen, the time seemed right to take a

Another Gold for Heddle and McBean!

break. She wanted to get away from the physical and mental demands of training day after day. So she decided to retire. But Marnie wasn't finished yet. She wanted to continue her career.

Over the next two years, Marnie rowed by herself much of the time. And she rowed in a different kind of boat. When she was rowing pairs, she used only one oar. Now she rowed alone in a scull. So she had to learn to use two oars.

Marnie worked hard learning to row by herself. She became very good, winning a silver medal in the singles scull event at the 1993 World Championships. But she missed her old partner. She missed being part of a team. And she missed having someone to train with.

In 1994, Marnie got on the phone and called Kathleen. She wanted her to come back to rowing. Kathleen agreed, but she wanted to do something different. They

decided that instead of rowing together in a pairs boat, they would row together in a scull. The change made sense. They had won all they could as pairs rowers — Canadian and world championships and Olympic gold. It was time for something new.

Soon the two were winning all the scull races. As the 1996 Atlanta Olympics came close, the Canadian rowing team was very strong. Hopes were high for the whole team, including Kathleen and Marnie.

July 27, 1996, was race day. Three teams would try for gold — the Canadians, the Chinese and the Dutch.

There had been strong head winds for most of the training week. Kathleen and Marnie prepared themselves to deal with the wind, but it died down before race day. They would just have to adapt their stroke rate. They could hardly wait for the race to begin.

"Start!" They were off! No more nerves. Just 2000 metres of hard work.

Marnie and Kathleen took the lead early and continued to build on it until about halfway through the race. Then they started to feel pressure from the Chinese and Dutch crews. With 500 metres to go, the race was a close one. The Canadians were giving it all they had. Marnie later said that she felt as though they were "on the very edge, moments away from having nothing left."

Thousands of fans were on their feet cheering for the two Canadians. They were calling to the pair to hold on as their boat sped toward the finish line. Kathleen and Marnie continued to push themselves. Their muscles burned with pain. Two hundred metres . . . 150 metres . . .

The cheers were getting louder! Fifty metres . . . Where was the finish line? Twenty metres . . . 10 metres . . . finish line! It was over at last. Kathleen and Marnie were Olympic champions!

It was the first time Canadians had ever won a gold medal in an Olympic sculling event. It was also the third Olympic gold medal for both women. No Canadian in any sport had ever won three gold medals at the Olympics. Kathleen and Marnie stood side by side on the podium. Their medals dangled from their necks as they sang "O Canada."

Two weeks later, the Canadian Olympic Association asked Olympic organizers for a special favour. Usually they choose one athlete to carry the Canadian flag during the closing ceremonies. They asked if two people could carry it this time.

So, on the last day of the Olympics, Marnie McBean and Kathleen Heddle walked into the stadium together. They carried the Canadian flag proudly. It was another first for one of rowing's great partnerships!

1996

Donovan Bailey Fastest Man in the World!

One of the track and field events that people look forward to most at the Summer Olympics is the men's 100 metre final. It's a short race. It takes about as much time to run it as it takes you to write your name and address. But the winner gets the title of "fastest man in the world." Canadian Donovan Bailey won that title at the 1996 Olympics in Atlanta.

Donovan did track and field at high school in Oakville, Ontario. His long legs and great speed helped him win in the sprinting events. At the high school championships, he ran the men's 100 metre final in 10.65 seconds.

When Donovan left high school, he went to college to study business. He got away from running until 1991, when he decided to return to the track. As he said years later, "I didn't want to get older and regret not doing something I could have been good at."

After two years of hard work, Donovan began to believe he was good enough to think about becoming an Olympic athlete. At the Canadian Track and Field Championships in 1993, he came in third in the 100 metre race and second in the 200 metres.

That meant he could join the Canadian "4x100" relay team. In the 4x100, each of the four team members runs 100 metres before passing the baton to the next runner.

A trip to the World Track and Field Championships in Germany was the turning point in Donovan's career. He ran against the world's best runners, but they weren't much better than he was. His running caught the eye of coach Dan Pfaff.

Dan could see how good Donovan was. He told the young runner that, if he worked hard, he could be one of the best in the world. Donovan decided that he would quit everything else he was doing and give it a shot.

In 1994 he worked harder than he ever had before. And his new coach pushed him to work even harder. Donovan loved it. He had started out to "give it a shot." Now he was a world-class runner.

At the 1995 Canadian Championships, he ran well. His winning time for the 100 metre race was 9.91 seconds — the fastest time in the world that year, and the fourth fastest time ever!

Everybody thought he would shine at that year's World Track and Field Championships in Sweden. And he did. He won two gold medals. He won the 100 metres in 9.97 seconds. And he helped Canada's 4x100 team win first place.

The Atlanta Olympics was only a year away. Donovan wanted to be ready. He also wanted to try to break the 100 metre world record. American Leroy Burrell held that record. It was 9.85. That was .06 of a second better than the fastest time Donovan had ever run.

That small .06 may not sound like much. But in a 100 metre race, the difference between first place and last place can be .5 of a second. That's about as long as it takes you to blink your eye! So .06 can make a big difference.

During the 1996 indoor season, Donovan kept working toward his goal of Olympic gold. He won eight of the nine races he ran. And he set a world indoor record in the 50 metre with a time of 5.56 seconds. He was in top form. Everybody was expecting great things from him at the Olympics.

Race night in Atlanta was July 27, 1996. It was hot and humid. The stadium was packed. The eight fastest men in the world made their way onto the track:

- In lane one was Mike Marsh of the United States. He more often ran in the 200 metre, but he was also a fine 100 metre runner.

- In lane two was defending Olympic champion Linford Christie of Britain.

- In lane three was Ato Bolden of Trinidad and Tobago. He was a good starter who had come in with a time of 9.95.

- In lane four was American Dennis Mitchell. He usually started very quickly, but he often slowed down as the race went on.

- In lane five was Frankie Fredericks of Namibia. He had come in with a 9.93 and would push Donovan hard.

- Donovan was in lane six.

- In lane seven was Davidson Ezinwa of Nigeria.

- Michael Green of Jamaica was in lane eight. He, too, was a fast starter.

The racers got ready. The words came from the starter: "Ready . . . set . . ." The starter's pistol cracked. Another crack quickly followed. It was a false start. Linford had started a little before the gun went off.

They lined up again. There was another false start. This time Ato had moved before the gun went off. They tried a third time. Again a runner jumped the gun. It was Linford! Because this was his second false start, he was out of the race. He argued with the officials, but finally left the track. The other racers got ready for a fourth try.

"Ready . . . set . . ." Bang! This time they were off. Ato and Frankie were in front. Donovan was in fifth place as they hit the 40 metre mark. Then he began to speed up. He flew past the other runners, and by the 60 metre mark he was in first place.

It was hard to believe how fast they were running as they headed towards the finish line. Thousands cheered. Millions watched

on television around the world. When the race ended, it was Donovan in front. He had a world-record time of 9.84 seconds! Frankie was second with a 9.89. Ato was third with a 9.90. Donovan was only .06 of a second ahead of the third-place runner.

Donovan Bailey was the first Canadian ever to win the men's Olympic 100 metre race. He was the "fastest man in the world." And, at that moment, he was the happiest man in the world!

1997

Ted Nolan Wins Coach of the Year!

It was the end of the 1997 hockey season. Ted Nolan stood to receive the Jack Adams Trophy, the National Hockey League (NHL) award for Coach of the Year. This honour followed years of hard work.

Ted is a member of the Ojibway tribe. He grew up on the Garden River Indian Reservation just outside Sault Ste. Marie, Ontario. Like most kids in Canada, Ted loved to play hockey. Because his family was poor, he didn't have proper hockey equipment. But he would play for hours — working on his skills and just having fun.

People soon noticed that Ted had the skill to do more than simply play for fun. A team in Kenora, Ontario, invited him to join them. He was excited to be playing for a real team. But his family was a close one, and he was unhappy about having to leave home.

Ted was only 16 years old when he headed off to Kenora. It was tough being away from home for the first time. For the first few weeks, he wondered if he'd done the right thing. It was especially hard when he had to endure racist remarks. As a native Canadian, he became the target of some players on other teams and some narrow-minded fans.

Ted continued to improve as a player. Soon he moved closer to home with a spot on the Sault Ste. Marie Greyhounds in the Ontario Hockey League. He played with the Greyhounds for two seasons. One of his teammates during his second season was Wayne Gretzky.

In 1978, the Detroit Red Wings picked Ted in the entry draft. He was 20 years old,

and an NHL career awaited him. But he
would have to play in the minor leagues for a
few years. And life in the minor leagues can
be tough. For a while Ted wondered if all the
hard work and sacrifice were worthwhile. His
mother was the one who urged him not to
give up on his dream.

He spent three and a half seasons
playing in the minors, mostly with the
Adirondack Red Wings in the American
Hockey League. Finally, in the 1981-82
season, Ted got his chance with the Detroit
Red Wings. He played 41 games with them
and managed 17 points. He was happy that
he was finally getting his chance in the big
leagues. But just after he broke into the
NHL, he got sad news — his mother had
been killed by a drunk driver.

Keeping in mind his mother's support,
Ted kept working to become a full-time
player in the NHL. But over the next four

seasons he appeared in only 27 games, some with the Red Wings and some with the Pittsburgh Penguins. Then, in 1986, he was forced to retire because of a back injury.

Still only in his late 20s, Ted found himself, wondering what to do next. He had always been interested in the lives of native Canadians. Perhaps he could do something to help them if he went into politics? Or maybe he could make a difference as a police officer? But, even though his playing career had come to an end, he still loved hockey. So he turned to coaching.

Ted joined the Sault Ste. Marie Greyhounds as assistant coach. Part way through the 1988-89 season, he took over as head coach. The Greyhounds were a struggling team when Ted took over. They continued to struggle through the following season. But in 1990-91, they finished the season with a record of 42 wins, 21 losses

and 3 ties. They won the Ontario Hockey
League title.

By winning the title, the Greyhounds
earned the right to play in the Memorial
Cup tournament for the National Junior
Championship. It was the first of three trips
to that tournament in three years. Twice they
were league champions. The third time, in
1993, they were the host team and received
an automatic place in the tournament.

That year, the final game was played on
a muggy Sunday in May. In front of a
national television audience and a jam-
packed arena, the Greyhounds defeated the
Peterborough Petes. As the last few seconds
clicked off the clock, Ted jumped for joy
behind the bench. His team was finally about
to win a Memorial Cup title. To this day that
remains one of the proudest moments of his
hockey career.

After his success as a coach in junior

hockey, it seemed natural for Ted to take an NHL coaching job. He spent the 1994-95 season as assistant coach with the Hartford Whalers. Then, in July of 1995, he became head coach of the Buffalo Sabres. He had a lot to learn in his first season as head coach, and he threw himself into the challenge.

"My first year was everything I thought it would be, and a little bit more," recalls Ted. "Being a good coach is a growing process."

In his second season, Ted was a little more forceful. He insisted that the Sabres report to training camp in top shape. He pushed them to be a more aggressive team. They responded with a great effort all season. They went from a fifth-place team to a first-place team. They increased their point total by 19. They earned respect from the other teams as a tough opponent.

Ted also won respect. People saw him as a coach who could motivate his players and

get the most out of them. Buffalo didn't have as much talent as some teams, but they worked harder.

And the hard work paid off for Ted as well as the team. At the end of the season, he was voted NHL Coach of the Year!

Photo Credits

Front Cover: Canada's Sports Hall of Fame,
(inset) Stan Behal/*The Toronto Sun*
Back Cover: (top) National Archives of Canada
Negative No. C 014065, (bottom) *The Toronto Sun*
1, 3: National Archives of Canada Negative No.
C 014065
5: National Archives of Canada Negative No.
PA 051560
9, 11: Canada's Sports Hall of Fame
15: Canada's Sports Hall of Fame
17, 19: Canapress/Frank Lennon
21: Hockey Hall of Fame
25: Lori Fung
27: Lori Fung
29: Canadian Sport Images
33,35: John Gibson
39: Canapress
41,45: *The Toronto Sun*
42: (both) Julien LeBourdais/ *The Toronto Sun*
49,51: Canadian Wheelchair Basketball Association
55: Canadian Wheelchair Basketball Association
57,59: Miles Nadal/ Hockey Hall of Fame
61: Doug MacLellan/ Hockey Hall of Fame